Jennifer Lawrence
BURNING BRIGHT

Katy Sprinkel

TRIUMPH
BOOKS

This book is available in quantity at special discounts for your group or organization. For further information, contact:

Triumph Books LLC
814 North Franklin Street
Chicago, Illinois 60610
(312) 337-0747
www.triumphbooks.com

Printed in U.S.A.

ISBN: 978-1-60078-907-6

Content developed and packaged by Rockett Media, Inc.
Written by Katy Sprinkel
Edited by Bob Baker
Design and page production by Patricia Frey
Cover design by Andrew Burwell

All photos courtesy of Getty Images unless otherwise noted.

Jennifer Lawrence
BURNING BRIGHT

CHAPTER ONE
GROWING UP JEN

On August 15, 1990, in Louisville, Kentucky, a star was born. Parents Gary and Karen Lawrence, along with sons Ben and Blaine, welcomed little Jennifer to the world with open arms.

Jennifer, known as "Jen" to friends and family, had by all counts a typical and happy upbringing. Raised in suburban Louisville, her father owned a contracting business. Her mother ran Camp Hi-Ho, a rural retreat for nearby city kids.

The first girl on the Lawrence side of the family in 50 years, it's little wonder Jennifer grew up a self-described tomboy. Indeed, her parents were

Jennifer hanging out with (left to right) Alex Black, Shanica Knowles, and Tyler Neitzel at Tyler's 16th birthday party on September 30, 2007, in Los Angeles, California.

Jennifer Goes to the Movies

Jennifer admits she likes to go the dark, indie route in her roles, but her movie-watching tastes often veer toward mainstream fare.

Recalling her early movie memories, she told *W* magazine, "The first movie I ever saw was *Pocahontas*. I saw it like eight or nine times in the theater. But that's because I didn't know that any other movies were in movie theaters," she added, cheekily.

Her tastes soon gravitated toward broad comedies such as *Planes, Trains and Automobiles* and *There's Something About Mary*. She claims to have every line from *Anchorman* and *Dumb & Dumber* committed to memory ("Go on, give me a scene," she urged reporter Lynn Hirshberg, before knocking Jim Carrey's ode to Aspen from *Dumb & Dumber* out of the park).

But it's not just comedies that float her boat. She also loves romance. She admits she's seen *Bridget Jones's Diary* more than 50 times. What's a surefire way to make the actress cry? Just put on *Love Actually.*

A young Jennifer already looks the part of a California girl.

insistent their little girl have some fight in her, raising her just as they did her older brothers. "I didn't want her to be a diva," Karen Lawrence once said. "I didn't mind if she was girly, as long as she was tough."

More interested in dirt than dresses, Jennifer was often outside playing sports or spending time with her family's horses. "Growing up, I lived 15 minutes away from [my family's] horse farm, and I went there almost every day," she told *Seventeen* magazine. "My brothers were into fishing, but I was all about the horses."

Her first horse was a female pony named Muffin. "She was cute, but... mean," Jennifer told *Rolling Stone*. Later, she had two male horses, Dan and Brumby. "Those two hated each other," she continued, "but then one day there was a big storm and they spent the night huddled in the barn together, and suddenly they were inseparable."

Jennifer typically rode bareback, since most of the tack in the family's barn belonged to others who boarded their horses there. "I just kind of hopped on and went for it," she told an

> ## Some people think I missed out, but if I had the choice of being in class or moving to New York, I got the childhood of my dreams."
>
> — Jennifer on her decision to graduate early from high school, to *Teen Vogue*

Jennifer at the 2013 Film Independent Spirit Awards, accompanied by brothers Ben and Blaine

incredulous David Letterman in 2011. Her horses were untrained, which might explain why she was injured so often while riding them. She hurt her elbow jumping off a wildly galloping horse at one point, and fractured her tailbone at another.

The only girl in the house, she took cues from her brothers growing up. It was from Ben and Blaine that she got her early movie education, which was heavy on comedy. By age five she was parroting bits from *Billy Madison* and *Saturday Night Live*. "I got all of their hand-me-downs, so I was watching *MacGyver* and listening to Vanilla Ice," she told *Louisville* magazine.

She also endured more than her fair share of ribbing from her older brothers, something that continues today. Now an A-list movie star, she admits her brothers keep her grounded. "They don't care…. They just keep telling me I'm ugly." They're joking of course, but it helps her keep the whole fame thing in perspective.

by the NUMBERS

6

The number of years Jen spent cheerleading before pursuing a new interest: acting!

Jennifer earned her childhood nickname "Nitro" because of her seemingly limitless energy. Indeed, her middle school classmates named her "Most Talkative." As a teenager, she was involved in everything from cheerleading and dance to field hockey and softball. She even played basketball on a team her dad coached. (Fun fact: Gary Lawrence cameos in a future film as, you guessed it, Jennifer's basketball coach.)

Perhaps all that boundless energy made her restless in the classroom.

"I hated it. I hated being inside. I hated being behind a desk. School just kind of killed me," she told the *Los Angeles Times.* "I always felt dumber than everybody else," she continued, revealing that a teacher once embarrassed her in front of the class when she did not grasp a math assignment.

A veteran of church plays, Jennifer admits that she first cut her acting teeth getting out of trouble in school. Once, she received a suspension for jumping out of the back door of a bus but pleaded her case with the principal, telling him (with great exaggeration) that she was afraid for her life! Not only did the administrator drop the suspension, but she received two weeks homework-free for post-traumatic stress. That must have been some performance!

Despite her admissions of struggling in class, Jennifer was a very good student—good enough to graduate on the honor roll with a 3.9 grade point average. Not only that, but she graduated two years early, paving the way for her acting career.

Motivated to give modeling and acting a try, Jennifer convinced her mom to travel to New York City during the summer, so that the then-14-year-old Jennifer could meet with agents and (hopefully) go on auditions.

> **It was the first time I had that feeling like *I understand this. This is the first time I've ever understood anything.*"**
>
> — Jennifer on realizing acting was her true calling

Proud parents Karen and Gary Lawrence with their daughter at the 2013 Academy Awards.

As luck would have it, fate intervened on their very first day. As Jennifer stood with her mom, watching breakdancers perform in Union Square, a talent agent spotted her in the crowd and asked if he could take her picture. "I had no idea that was creepy," she later told *Rolling Stone*. Luckily, the photographer was a legitimate model scout. The very next day, she was meeting agents and heading out on auditions. "One of them gave me a script, to audition the next day, and I read the script and it was the first time I had that feeling like *I understand this. This is the first time I've ever understood anything*," she told *Vanity Fair*.

Now all she needed to do was convince her parents, who were far from the typical stage parents, to let her pursue her new dream. They were not too keen on her becoming an actress. But a determined Jennifer convinced them that she was serious about it, and they relented. She could stay through the summer—with her mother, of course—but she had to come home again before school started.

It became evident very soon that she had something special when she got a callback on her *very first audition*. She didn't get the job, but auditions soon began to hit—a commercial here, a photo call there. Before long, no less than Hollywood came calling.

Is it any wonder this face stood out from the crowd?

Sure, you know everything there is to know about Katniss, Raven, and Tiffany—but what about the *real* Jennifer? Test your knowledge of Jennifer before she hit the big time with this brain-busting quiz.

1. What's her favorite basketball team?

a) Kentucky Wildcats

b) Louisville Cardinals

c) Duke Blue Devils

d) Tennessee Volunteers

2. She was a cheerleader for Kammerer Middle School. What is their mascot?

a) Eagles

b) Pirates

c) Raiders

d) Cubs

3. Which unusual pet did she have growing up?

a) goat

b) ferret

c) snake

d) sugar glider

4. She has an uncommon middle name. What is it?

a) Sargent

b) Baxter

c) Shrader

d) Bexley

5. Which of these fellow actors is NOT a native Kentuckian?

a) Josh Hutcherson

b) Shia LaBeouf

c) Johnny Depp

d) George Clooney

6. Which book series was Jennifer obsessed with as a young girl?

a) *The Baby-Sitters Club*

b) *Nancy Drew*

c) *The Chronicles of Narnia*

d) *Harry Potter*

7. Which boy band was she crushing on back in the day?

a) Backstreet Boys

b) Hanson

c) N*SYNC

d) 98 Degrees

Answers:

CHAPTER TWO

CALIFORNIA DREAMIN'

Jen shouted out to MTV in her 2013 Screen Actors Guild Award acceptance speech.

After that fateful summer in New York, Jennifer was hooked. "When I first got to New York, my feet hit the sidewalk and you'd have thought I was born and raised there. I took over that town. None of my friends took me seriously. I came home and announced, 'I'm going to move to New York,' and they were like 'Okay.' Then when I did, they kept waiting for me to fail and come back. But I knew I wouldn't. I was like, 'I'll show you,'" she told the *Guardian*.

And show them she did. Determined to make a mark as an actress, Jennifer hit the ground running. With a talent agency secured, she started pounding the pavement, attending audition after audition, just like any hopeful actress.

By her own estimation, she wasn't great in the beginning, but before long, something hit. So what *was* Jennifer's first job? Chances are, if you were watching MTV in 2005, you saw a star in the making. She was cast as the lead in promos for the network's smash reality series *My Super Sweet 16*, which profiles the over-the-top, outsized birthday parties for its overindulged 16-year-old subjects. In the promos, a spoiled Lisa (Jennifer) gets her comeuppance when her cake gets smashed and she gets dropped on her rear end! For a tomboy from Kentucky, playing a nasty little rich girl might have been a stretch, but she played the part of a mean girl perfectly.

Years later, when she won her first Screen Actors Guild Award, she namechecked those MTV commercials in her acceptance speech: "I want to thank

"I just love movies with teeth. I love movies that make you think."

— Jennifer on what she responds to in a script

MTV. I'll explain that. I earned my SAG card when I was 14. I did an MTV promo for *My Super Sweet 16*. And I remember getting it in the mail and it being the best day in my entire life, because it officially made me a professional actor."

More work soon followed, including national commercial campaigns for Burger King and print modeling gigs (including an Abercrombie & Fitch campaign in which her "flared nostrils" left her on the cutting-room floor).

Perhaps it's fitting that the first big break for this Kentucky girl came from one of the biggest Southern-fried comedians in the business: Blue Collar Comedy all-star Bill Engvall. Still relatively unproven, Jennifer was cast in a lead role in the comedian's *The Bill Engvall Show*. The TBS sitcom centered on the Pearson family: father Bill (Engvall) and mother Susan (played by Nancy Travis, a comedy stalwart from films like *So I Married an Axe Murderer*), and three children. Jennifer played Lauren Pearson, a sassy but sensitive teenager who occasionally likes to push her parents' buttons.

The program showcased the actress' blooming talent, especially her crackerjack comic timing and skill as a physical comedian. The family comedy, filmed in front of a live studio audience, played for a lot of laughs. But it was also a values-based show that tackled some serious issues. As such, she also got to show her sensitive side.

Speaking to Kentucky's MetroMix in 2012, Engvall said, "Of my favorite scenes that I did on that show, one of

this day in HER-STORY

July 17, 2007

The Bill Engvall Show premieres on TBS, and America meets Jennifer Lawrence.

Jennifer and her TV
family: (clockwise from
left) Graham Patrick
Martin, Bill Engvall, and
Skyler Gisondo

Jennifer, director Lori Petty, and co-star Selma Blair premiere *The Poker House* at the 2008 Los Angeles Film Festival.

> **I remember [thinking],**
> *This girl's good. She's got it;*
> *she's got what it takes."*
>
> — Bill Engvall on recognizing
> Jennifer's innate talent

them was with Jennifer. I go back and watch it every once in a while. We had a scene where she was mad at me and I had to go in and apologize to her. We had that nice dad-daughter moment. I remember [thinking], *This girl's good. She's got it; she's got what it takes."*

The show provided Jennifer with her first steady paycheck, and it was fertile training ground for her as a young actress. Because of the show's shooting schedule, she was also able to pursue other work on the side. She had a memorable turn as a young Allison Dubois on *Medium* and landed a guest spot on *Cold Case*, among other gigs.

"*The Bill Engvall Show*, I'm so grateful for it," Lawrence said. "I had so much fun on that show, and we all became like family. It funded my indie career, so I could do the movies that I want," she told *Under the Radar* magazine.

Her first movie role was in 2008's *The Poker House*. It was the first in a string of gritty, independent dramas to which Jennifer would gravitate. She played Agnes, the eldest of three daughters living in a broken home frequented by drug dealers, pimps, and other criminals. The role posed a unique challenge for Jennifer: she was playing a real-life subject. Co-writer and first-time director Lori Petty based the script on her own

Personality TEST

Name: Agnes

Age: 14

Hometown: Council Bluffs, Iowa

Likes: basketball, cleanliness, soul music

Dislikes: mice, violence, dishonesty

How you go from here to there: on my bike

Favorite subject: English

Hidden talent: writing poetry

Philosophy: "I race the sun home in the morning, and the moon up at night. There's just today, and then there's tonight. Anything can happen, then anything does. You get through it."

Fun fact: I share a birthday with e.e. cummings

difficult childhood. Considering the very personal nature of the film, Petty felt the casting of the lead role was crucial. "Jennifer blew everyone away. There was Jennifer, and then there was everyone else," Petty said.

Lawrence appeared in virtually every scene of the movie. It was a grueling, by-the-shoestrings independent shoot. "It's Jennifer's film. Jennifer carries this movie on her back; it's her movie," Petty continued. The actress and the movie earned accolades from critics across the nation. "*The Poker House* works because its indomitable 14-year-old heroine, Agnes, is so acutely well-drawn and so beautifully played by Jennifer Lawrence…. [Lawrence's] shining portrayal is ably supported by a fine cast in this vital, stirring film," wrote the *Los Angeles Times* in its review. She also won Best Performance at the Los Angeles Film Festival.

"I just love movies with teeth. I love movies that make you think. I love

Jennifer with *The Burning Plain* director Guillermo Arriaga and co-star Charlize Theron at the 65th Venice Film Festival.

movies that are going to challenge me," she told *Acted By* magazine.

Her role in 2008's *The Burning Plain* certainly had teeth. In the psychological drama by Guillermo Arriaga (*Amores Perros, Babel*), Jennifer held her own alongside Oscar-winners Charlize Theron and Kim Basinger. Theron, who also produced the movie, told *Entertainment Weekly* she was "crushed into silence" when she first watched Lawrence's audition tape. "When we first met in person, it was so clear that this girl was going to take over the world," she said.

It was with this film that Jennifer got her first taste of real Hollywood glamour when the movie premiered on the sun-splashed Adriatic coast at the Venice Film Festival. The movie was well received, and Jennifer took home the Marcello Mastroianni Award for Best Young Actress at the festival.

She couldn't have known it then, but an even bigger success was right around the corner.

Match each quote below with the character (played by Jennifer, of course!) who said it.

1. "Lots of things are wrong, Momma, and they can't be fixed by praying."

2. "I'm a teenager. I don't have time!"

3. "Lock your doors at night. That's what I do."

4. "I remember when I was 10 somebody gave me a diary for a present. But I felt like it was too late, so I didn't write in it. Too much had already happened. So, it wouldn't be the whole story."

A. Lauren Pearson (*The Bill Engvall Show*)

B. Mariana (*The Burning Plain*)

C. Agnes (*The Poker House*)

D. Tiff (*Garden Party*)

Answers:

1-B, 2-A, 3-D, 4-C

A beaming Jen takes home the Marcello Mastroianni Award for Best Young Actress at the 2008 Venice Film Festival.

CHAPTER THREE
REE, DISCOVERED

After three seasons on the air, *The Bill Engvall Show* faded quietly into the television twilight. It was a turning point for Jennifer, who had until that point been performing a balancing act between TV and movies. On the one hand, she was losing a day job; on the other, she could now pursue her film career full-time.

One of the last films that Jennifer shot during the *Engvall* era was a little indie about an Ozark teenager fighting for her family's survival. It was a quiet little story, but it was powerful. Jennifer was attracted to the prospect immediately.

Kathy Lawrence was the first one to steer her daughter to the project, based

The cast of *Winter's Bone.*

Jen looks radiant at the Film Independent screening of *Winter's Bone* in 2010.

Jen and co-star/pal Lauren Sweetser celebrate the American Film Institute's inclusion of *Winter's Bone* in its Year of Excellence.

"**Lawrence is the movie's blooming discovery, a mesmerizing actor with a gaze that's the opposite of actress-coy and a voice modulated in the low, almost monotone cadences of local ways.**"

— Lisa Schwartzbaum, in her *Entertainment Weekly* review of *Winter's Bone*

on Daniel Woodrell's 2007 novel *Winter's Bone*. "My mom read the book five, some six years ago. And when she read it, she said, 'Jennifer, if they ever make this into a movie, you'd be perfect for it.' And you know, I didn't listen to her, because she's my mother, but five years later I got the script and the audition," Jennifer said.

There were scores of hopefuls up for the part, and the audition process was lengthy. Jennifer auditioned twice in Los Angeles before finding out they thought she looked too polished for the part. "I'd

have walked on hot coals to get the part. I thought it was the best female role I'd read—ever. I was so impressed by Ree's tenacity and that she didn't take no for an answer. For the [third] audition, I had to fly on the red-eye to New York and be as ugly as possible. I didn't wash my hair for a week, I had no makeup on. I looked beat up in there. I think I had icicles hanging from my eyebrows." Perhaps it was the icicles, but more likely it was her sheer determination—a central character trait for Ree. Whatever it was, the part was hers.

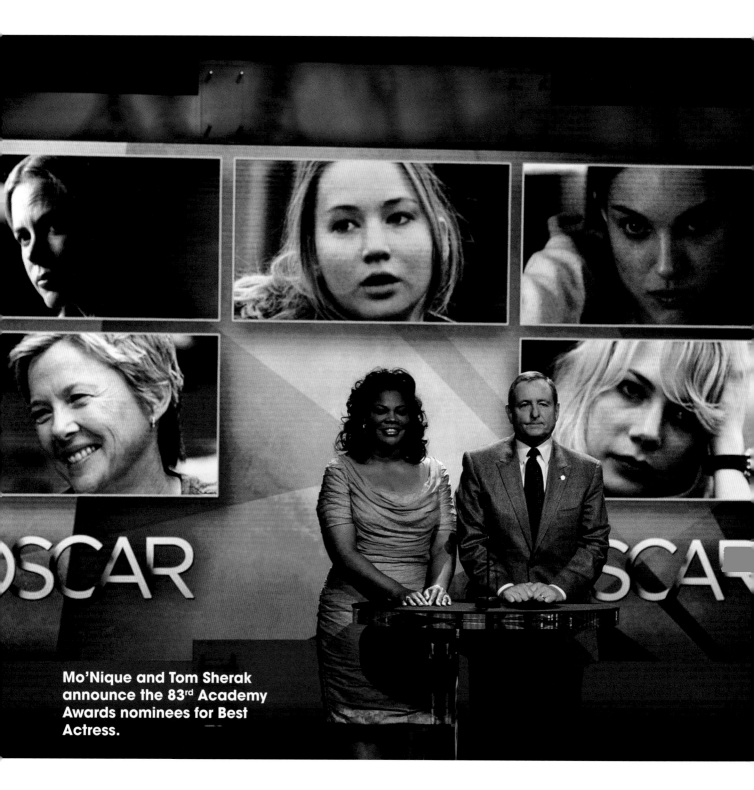

Mo'Nique and Tom Sherak announce the 83rd Academy Awards nominees for Best Actress.

The story is a sinister slice of Southern grit lit, a dark family drama about a young girl saddled with the very adult responsibilities of caring for her young siblings and catatonic mother. When Ree Dolly's absent father puts their house up for his bail bond and disappears, her family's fragile existence is threatened. That act sets in motion Ree's odyssean quest to find her father, dead or alive, against a bleak Missouri Ozark backdrop littered with drug addicts, criminals, and other unsavory folk—many of them kin.

Director Debra Granik (*Down to the Bone*), who developed the project and also co-wrote the script, was attracted to the story and its strong, female lead. "Ree's a character who isn't just stoic; she's got weak moments, she's got girlish moments, she's got more ordinary moments where she gets impatient with her brother and sister, and she's got kind moments. She can experience feelings that are very complicated for a young person," she said.

this day in HER-STORY

January 25, 2011

Jennifer is nominated for an Academy Award for her performance as Ree Dolly in *Winter's Bone*. At 20, she becomes the second-youngest actress ever nominated for the Best Actress Award, after 13-year-old Keisha Castle-Hughes in *Whale Rider*. (In 2013, Jennifer was knocked down to third all-time when nine-year-old Quvenzhané Wallis got a nod for her turn in *Beasts of the Southern Wild*. But true Jen fans know who took home the statuette *that* year!)

The shoot was guerilla filmmaking at its finest: no sets, a small crew, and a bare-bones budget. The film was shot on location in rural Missouri, and

Personality TEST

Name: *Ree Dolly*

Age: *17*

Hometown: *the Missouri Ozarks*

Nickname: *Sweet Pea*

Likes: *family, stability*

Dislikes: *chain saws, getting help from others*

Favorite subject: *ROTC*

Hidden talent: *expert markswoman*

How you go from here to there: *on foot*

Philosophy: *"Don't ask for what ought to be offered."*

Fun fact: *I can field dress a squirrel using only a pocketknife*

many locals, including Jennifer's on-screen sister, were cast in roles. It was a grueling six-week shoot that involved long hours, late nights, and the freezing cold.

Shot with no frills and with a small, $2 million budget, the filmmakers had modest expectations for its box-office success. But when the film premiered at the Sundance Film Festival in 2010, it blew festivalgoers away, winning the Grand Jury Prize for best film. "I just started bawling. I had such an 'actress' moment," Jennifer said of hearing the news. "I was there for the premiere of the movie, but then I went home [before the end of the festival].... And then Lauren Sweetser, who plays Gail in the movie—we became real-life best friends on the set and have been ever since—we called each other and just started screaming."

Heaps of critical praise soon followed. Reviewers were stunned by Jennifer and her performance, calling her "dazzling," "astounding,"

Jennifer attends the SAGIndie Actors Brunch during the 2010 Sundance Film Festival, at which *Winter's Bone* premiered—and ultimately took best

**Jennifer in
Winter's Bone.**

"I'd have walked on hot coals for that part."

— Jennifer on fighting for the role of
Ree in *Winter's Bone*

"luminous," and "a real discovery." The *Christian Science Monitor* went one better: "Jennifer Lawrence [is] probably the most gifted actress of her generation. How wonderful that so young, she has already found a role worthy of her talent."

The film grossed $16 million worldwide—not quite blockbuster numbers, but between the healthy box office and the review attention, the indie was an unmitigated success. "I mean none of us did it for the money!... We didn't do it for any other reason than we loved that film. And everybody, the crew included, were all really

passionate about this project," Jennifer said.

For Jennifer, the attention was welcome, if a little surprising. "I learned that you can't have any expectations with life or with this business. *The Burning Plain* was a million-dollar movie with huge movie stars, and everybody was convinced that [it] was going to be huge and that [it] was my star-making role. Every movie that has come out has been my 'breakthrough role.' Then *Winter's Bone*—the one that was a hundred dollars to make, tiny, and everybody thought it will be fun but nobody will ever see it—has gotten huge. You never know what's going to happen," she told the *Huffington Post* in early 2011.

The movie may have been "huge" then, but what happened next was even huger. The 2011 Academy Awards were buzzing with highbrow studio fare like *The King's Speech*, *The Social Network*, and *Black Swan*. But it was the little indie that could that made one of the biggest splashes when Jennifer received a dark-horse nomination for Best Actress. The award pitted her against the likes of Hollywood heavyweights (and all previous Oscar nominees) Annette Bening, Nicole Kidman, Natalie Portman, and Michelle Williams.

With *Winter's Bone*, Jennifer had arrived. Seemingly overnight, she had become a household name.

A short two years later, accepting an Independent Spirit Award for her role in *Silver Linings Playbook*, Jennifer reflected on her roots in independent film, and especially why *Winter's Bone* was so special to her. "The vibe on *that* set was exactly what makes me love indies. The only reason we were all out there in the freezing cold was because we loved the project. I *love* that feeling, that desperate, almost pathetic feeling of, 'Are we actually going to be able to pull this off?'"

Well, pull it off they did—big time.

I learned that you can't have any expectations with life or with this business."

— Jennifer on the attention she got from *Winter's Bone*, to the *Huffington Post*

Jen made quite an entrance at the 2011 Oscars. For those who knew her only as Ree Dolly, it was quite a transformation!

CHAPTER FOUR

KATNISS: A TRIBUTE

To describe Suzanne Collins' *Hunger Games* trilogy as popular would be... an understatement. The book series, encompassing *The Hunger Games* (2008), *Catching Fire* (2009), and *Mockingjay* (2010), has sold more than 50 million books, has been published in more than two dozen languages worldwide, and comprises the best-selling books *of all time* on Amazon.com, obliterating the record previously held by another popular YA book series— you know, the one involving a certain boarding school for wizards.

A runaway success in print, a movie adaptation quickly became a foregone conclusion. The question on everyone in Tinseltown's mind was, *Who will play Katniss Everdeen?* It seemed every young, high-profile actress wanted the part; Chloe Grace Moretz, Shailene Woodley, Saoirse Ronan, Emma Roberts, Abigail Breslin, and Hailee Steinfeld, among many others, all auditioned for the role. But according to director Gary Ross, there was one actress who stood out from the pack: Jennifer Lawrence.

"*The Hunger Games* is not that far off from real life. We are living in a world where we watch extreme-sports shows where people get hurt or killed. It takes a lot to shock us."

—Jennifer on the scary real-life parallels to *The Hunger Games* trilogy, to *Seventeen* magazine

Katniss Everdeen, District 12's female tribute. *Photo courtesy of AP Images*

The Hunger Games stars Josh Hutcherson, Jennifer, and Liam Hemsworth at the film's world premiere.

"I'd never seen an audition that good. Ever," he told MTV News. "I saw someone who I knew I was going to be watching for decades. Literally, I had the kind of moment where I stepped out and thought, *Okay, this is the beginning of a great acting career.*... That's honestly how I felt. She stunned me with the emotional depth of the audition."

It was Hollywood's most coveted role, but Jennifer was hesitant about saying yes. Having carved out a successful niche for herself within the independent film scene, a studio tentpole film like this one was a departure, to say the least. Not to mention the films, which would cover the entire book series, would span a number of years in her career.

"It's really rare that saying yes to something will completely change your life. I was happy with my life and I didn't know if I wanted it to change.... I took three days to decide, and each day was a different answer," she told *Fabulous* magazine.

did you KNOW?

Suzanne Collins has said that the idea for *The Hunger Games* trilogy was inspired by the Greek myth of Theseus, which made a lasting impression on the author when she first heard the tale as a young girl. In the myth, 12 Athenian boys and eight girls are sent every nine years against their will to fight the monstrous minotaur, a creature that is half-man and half-bull. The children are devoured and the cycle continues until the minotaur is slain at the hand of Theseus. Who said mythology was boring?!

Ultimately, it was Jen's mom, Karen, who helped her daughter make up her mind. She reminded her daughter that her decisions to commit to a film had never been about the size of the budget, but rather the quality of the role, the script, and the director. Jennifer loved the character of Katniss; to say no to *The Hunger Games* based on its size would be hypocrisy, pure and simple, Karen told her plainly. "So I said yes, and I haven't regretted it," the actress continued.

But some fans already attached to the book series and its central character objected to the choice, claiming Jennifer was not thin enough to play the starving, not to mention brunette, Katniss. But the movie was still in preproduction; fans would simply have to wait and see if Lawrence filled Katniss' shoes to their satisfaction. (Spoiler alert: she did!) Lawrence took the criticism in stride, later saying to *Elle*, "I'm never going to starve myself for a part. I don't want little girls to be like,

Oh, I want to look like Katniss, so I'm going to skip dinner.... I was trying to get my body to look fit and strong, not thin and underfed."

Fans certainly couldn't be disappointed by how much the actress loved Collins' book. "It was important to read the book because I imagined myself at a Q&A with people who loved the book. I love the *Twilight* books. I'm not even ashamed to say it—they are like methamphetamine to me. So when I heard Kristen Stewart say, 'I only read the first one,' I was like, *Oh, man,* because she wasn't a huge fan of the books. I was like, *For the book lovers I should probably read the books.*"

As the grueling preparations for filming began, Jennifer began intensive training for her role as the expert archer. Olympic archer Khatuna Lorig schooled Jennifer on the finer points of the sport ("Isn't that what everybody does when they learn archery?" she joked to

Jennifer signs autographs for *THG* fans in L.A. The film's stars embarked on a nationwide publicity tour, meeting many fans face-to-face, before the movie's premiere.

Gale vs. Peeta: A Breakdown

Which side are you on: Team Peeta or Team Gale? Here's the breakdown on Katniss' leading men.

	Gale Hawthorne	Peeta Mellark
Appearance	Tall, dark, and handsome.	Fair and stocky.
Disposition	Tough.	Sweet.
Physical strength	Extreme; he's forced to depend on it, and his street smarts, for his own survival.	As a baker's son, he never needed much—until the Hunger Games!
Emotional availability	Gale's pretty closed off when it comes to his feelings.	Peeta is free with his affections. He even announced his feelings about Katniss on national television.
Achilles' heel	His recklessness.	His naivete.
Special connection with Katniss	They have known each other their whole lives.	They endured the Hunger Games together.

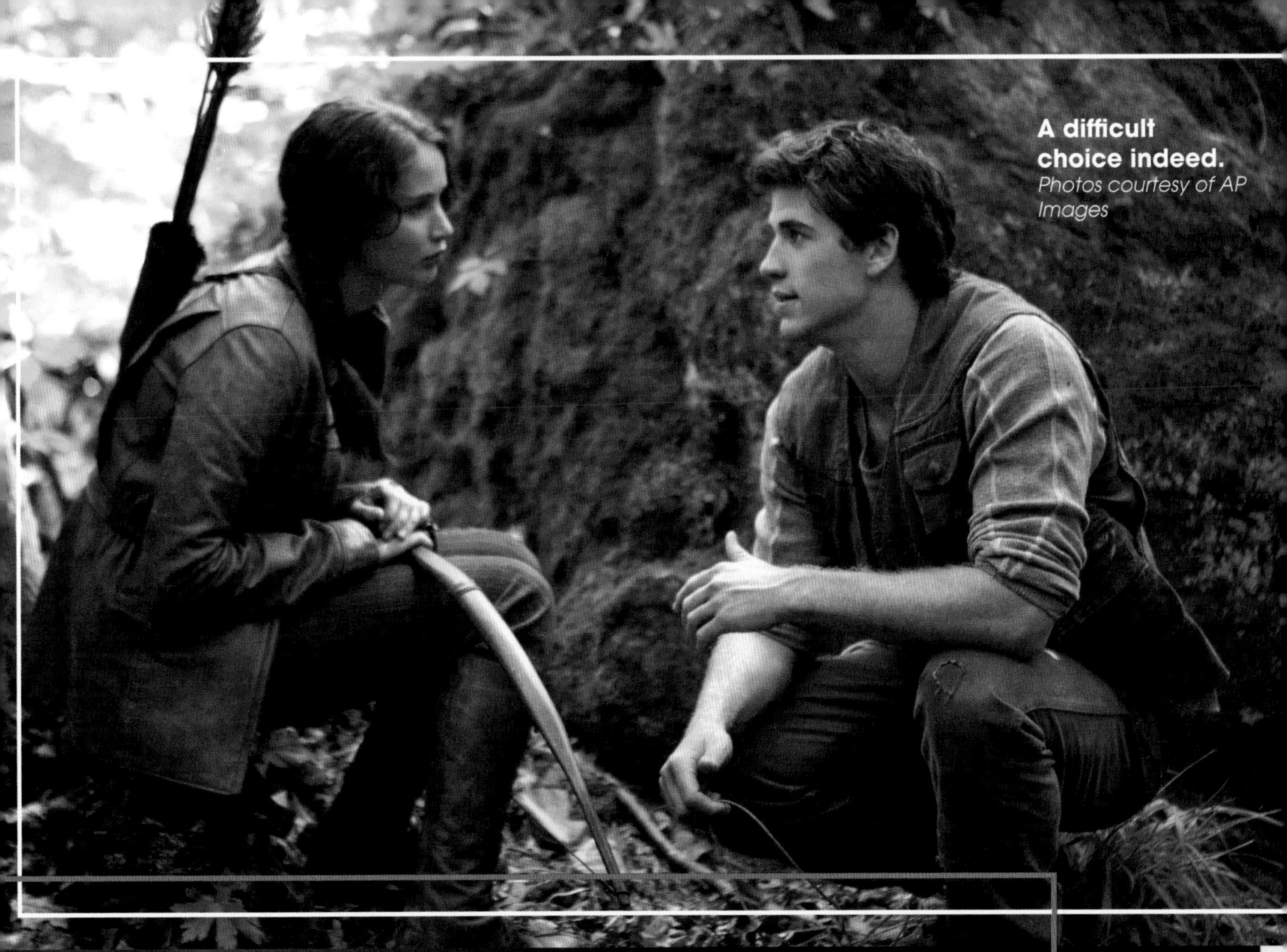

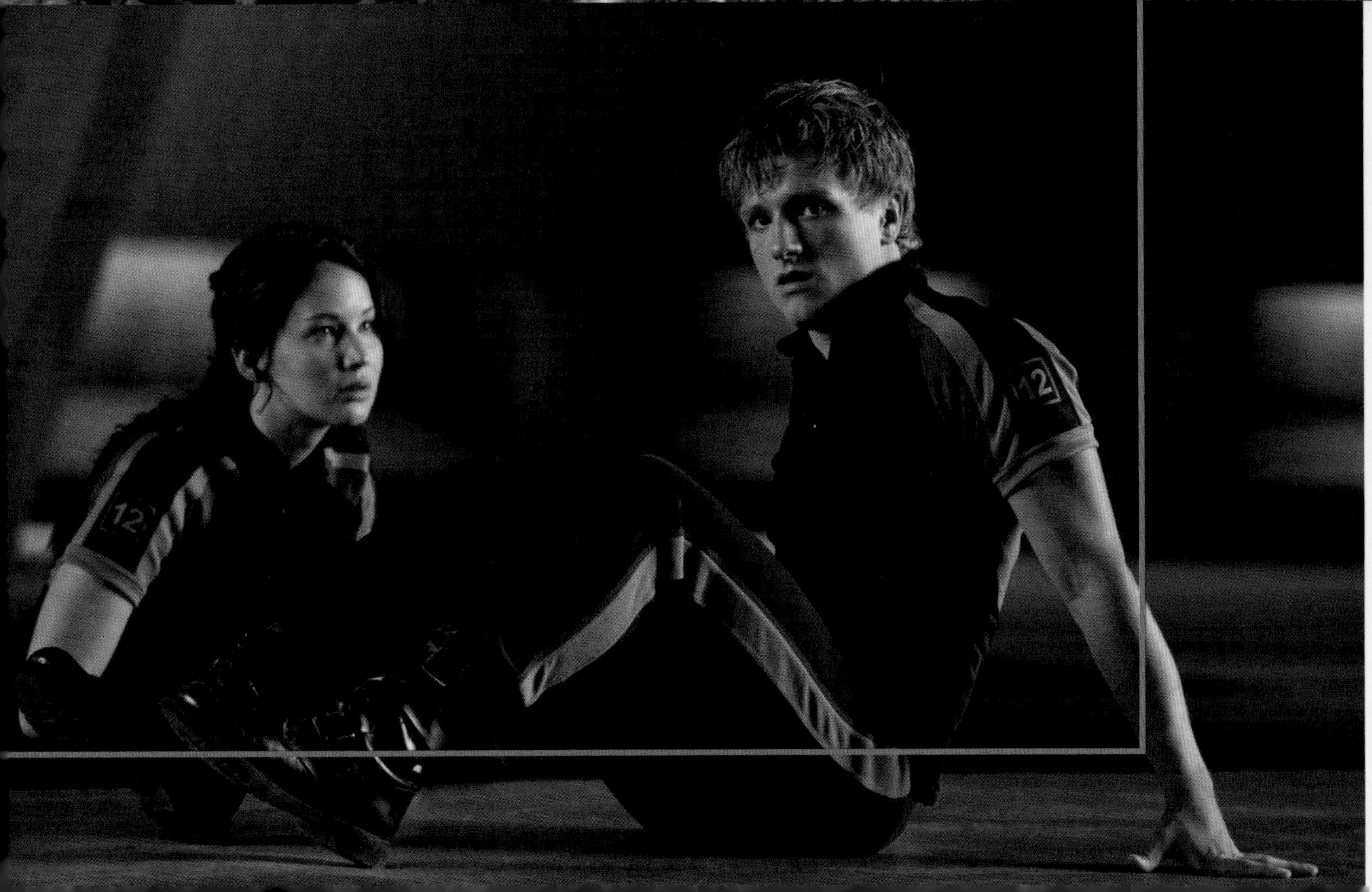

A difficult choice indeed.
Photos courtesy of AP Images

Personality TEST

Name: Katniss Everdeen

Age: 16

Hometown: The Seam, District 12, Panem

Nicknames: the Girl on Fire, the Mockingjay

Likes: hunting, horticulture

Dislikes: empty cupboards, bureaucracy

Hidden talent: my singing voice—the birds actually stop to listen! I'm pretty good with a bow and arrow, too.

How you get from here to there: on foot

Philosophy: "Keep calm and may the odds be ever in your favor."

Fun fact: My name saved my life once. (I'm named after an edible plant, so I found "myself" to stay alive.)

Chelsea Handler in 2012). Before long, Jennifer was shooting like a pro.

"Archery is a fun skill to have because it's nice to whip out at parties or photo shoots at any time and just [say] 'I could kill somebody.' It's painful to learn… The payoff of not paying attention is getting whipped inside the arm. But once you get the hang of it, it's pretty fun," she told *Glamour*.

In addition to archery, she also did daily workouts to improve her running technique, cardio workouts, and strength and conditioning exercises. She ran agility drills through an obstacle course created by the crew to mimic the wooded landscape of the Games. She also integrated yoga and even parkour into the mix!

If the preproduction training was a lot of work, the actual filming was even more involved. The movie—with a massive $80 million budget—was shot on location in North Carolina and had a little bit bigger production footprint than, say, some of Jennifer's previous

Jennifer signs autographs for fans of *Los Juegos del Hambre (The Hunger Games)* in Madrid.

Katniss takes aim. *Photo courtesy of AP Images*

films. Still, the production had the same comrades-at-arms feel as those indies she loves.

"In a lot of ways, filmmaking is like summer camp," she told the UK's *Sun*. "It's like a bunch of boys and girls away from their homes." So it was perhaps little surprise that the cast and crew pulled plenty of pranks along the way.

"Josh Hutcherson was the biggest prankster on set," she told *Seventeen*. In one of his best, he got a good scare out of Jennifer when he hid a prop dummy—one of the fallen tracker-jackers—inside her trailer's bathroom. "When she opened the door, she peed her pants. Or so I was told—I don't have visual confirmation on that one," he said. "It wasn't until I calmed down that I realized it was holding toilet paper in its hand, which made it even funnier," she told *Seventeen*.

All the laughs were tonic for the movie's somber tone. Collins' dystopian

Killer Instinct

What does an actress trained in the finer points of archery do when she thinks her house is being burglarized? Well, attack, of course! Describing the scene to *Vanity Fair*, she said, "I pulled into my garage and I heard men in my house. And I was like, *I'm not letting them take my stuff.* I had just gotten back from training, so I had the bow and arrows in the back of my car." She advanced upstairs, bowstring drawn, to discover…two men (legitimately) working on her patio. Crisis averted! Still, future crooks be forewarned. "That would be the funniest news ever," she laughed. "Katniss Everdeen actually kills someone with a bow and arrow!"

tale of teenagers forced to fight to the death is about as serious as it gets. And while Panem is a fictional place (thank goodness!) the story's themes still resonated with Jennifer. "*The Hunger Games* is not that far off from real life," she told *Seventeen*. "I think it's such an ugly truth about our world and it's such an interesting concept of history repeating itself and the brutality we have within all of us," she said to E!

Brutality aside, Katniss is also forced to contend with a battle of emotions: conflicting love interests in fellow tribute Peeta and hometown compatriot Gale. Portrayed by Hutcherson and Liam Hemsworth, respectively, Katniss was faced with quite a difficult choice.

Moviegoers flocked to the theaters when *The Hunger Games* premiered in March 2012. By all counts, it was a massive box-office success. The film had the third-highest debut in U.S. history. It went on to gross more than $400 million dollars in the U.S. and hundreds of millions more worldwide. What's more, critical reception was overwhelmingly positive.

There's absolutely no denying that the movie was a huge success in every respect. And with three more films in the pipeline, beginning with November 2013's *The Hunger Games: Catching Fire*, the *HG* train shows no signs of stopping. And those fans who thought Jennifer wasn't svelte enough to play their heroine? Like Katniss' observers in the Capitol, she's won them all over.

vocab CHECK

parkour (pär • kór) Invented in the urban environs outside Paris, parkour is a set of techniques that allow a participant to run, jump, roll, climb, or leap through any landscape with a minimum of wasted energy.

The Girl on Fire steps out
at the German premiere of
*Die Tribute die Panem—The
Hunger Games*, of course!

CHAPTER FIVE
OH NO SHE DIDN'T!

Jennifer goofing around on Spanish TV show *El Hormiguero* while promoting *The Hunger Games* in 2012.

"I never know what's going to come out of my mouth, and it's horrible," Jennifer told *Elle* magazine in 2012. It's a refreshing departure from today's Hollywood actresses, most of whom are strictly managed by teams of publicists, agents, managers, attorneys, studio executives, and a stable of other folks who all maneuver together to shape their "product." But it's precisely that unpredictability, that vulnerability, and that refusal to stick to a publicist's predetermined script that makes Jen's fans love her all the more. She's *real*, period.

"I would probably turn into a mute if I read what I said," she confessed to *Fabulous* magazine. But her honesty has won over people around the world. There are dozens of YouTube videos, some with millions of views, celebrating her gaffes and off-the-cuff remarks. Her one-liners have made her one of the most GIF-ed celebrities out there. Pop-culture website Vulture.com

she said WHAT?!

"In Hollywood, I'm obese."

To *Elle* magazine, talking about Hollywood's unrealistic perception of "normal"

runs a weekly "This Week in Jennifer Lawrence Quotes" feature. And what's more, considering the everybody's-a-critic nature of the Internet, negative commenters are nil; young, old, male, female—everyone loves this girl.

In today's viral world, where one verbal goof can sink a political campaign (here's looking at you, Rick Perry...Howard Dean...the list goes on) or, yes, even kill an actress' credibility (Kristen Stewart's admission that she had not read the *Twilight* books set off a wave of backlash among Twihards), being careful certainly has its virtues. One false step could kill a career... couldn't it?

Consider Jennifer's speech at the 2013 Golden Globes. Accepting the Best Actress in a Comedy or Musical Award, she rushed the stage and proudly exclaimed, "I beat Meryl!"

"I'm young, so I still have meltdown potential. Stay tuned."

Joking to the UK's *Sun* about staying grounded

(Actress Meryl Streep was a fellow nominee.) The comment left some scratching their heads, including Lindsay Lohan, who took to Twitter to admonish Jennifer for her insensitivity. *Had Jennifer just dissed the Grand Dame of Hollywood?* Jennifer laughed off the brouhaha. Speaking to David Letterman on *Late Show with David Letterman* the next evening, she said, "It's never a good idea for me to wing it, but it was a quote from *The First Wives Club....* I can't believe nobody has ever done it before...but Twitter is very upset." And with that, the "controversy" was quashed.

Perhaps it's no surprise that the woman who peppers acceptance speeches with movie references is pop-culture obsessed. The reality-TV-fixated star has repeatedly confessed her love for television as comfort food—everything from *Here Comes Honey Boo Boo* and *Keeping Up with the Kardashians* to *Jersey Shore* and

"I never know what's going to come out of my mouth, and it's horrible."

Jennifer does a little backpedaling backstage at the 2013 Oscars.

Intervention. (In fact, her love for Honey Boo Boo even caused her to crash her car. She got into a fender-bender when she mistook a random Georgia child for the famous pint-sized pageant queen!) She's even joked that TiVo ought to send her another receiver or two, considering how often she mentions the product on the red carpet (the device "changed my life," the actress opined). "At the end of the day, there's probably nothing that makes me feel better than junk food and reality TV," she told *Marie Claire South Africa.*

When she encountered fellow actress and interviewer Kristin Chenoweth on the Oscars red carpet in 2013, the two bubbled over about their shared love of *Dance Moms* and its central figure, authoritarian dance instructor Abby Lee Miller. In their excitement, one of them (guess who) might have gotten bleeped by the network for accidentally using a curse word. Whoops!

On the same red carpet, *Access Hollywood*'s Billy Bush showed Jennifer the just-printed glossies of her new Miss Dior ad. Suffice it to say, it probably wasn't the reaction the brand expected its spokeswoman to have. "Oh my God…that doesn't look like me at all. I love Photoshop more than anything in the world," she exclaimed. When the confused host tried to compliment the

she said
WHAT?!

"I'm sorry that I hit your family. I thought I just saw Honey Boo Boo."

Describing her apology after a minor car accident, on *The Tonight Show with Jay Leno*

she said WHAT?!

"Don't go see the movies. I'm a troll. I think the movie's great, but their biggest mistake was me."

Jennifer sarcastically promoting *The Hunger Games* on *Letterman*

"She'll say anything. *Anything*," *Hunger Games* co-star Lenny Kravitz told *Rolling Stone*. Fellow co-star Woody Harrelson's feelings are mutual: "She's the funniest woman I know." *THG* producer Nina Jacobson echoes them both, saying, "She's a goofball. She's fun and she's funny. She is the least demanding leading lady ever."

"The people I have worked with, mostly they don't really give advice; it's mostly just support and love…. I'm still waiting to get a couple tips on how to shut up," Jennifer told the press after the 2013 SAG Awards.

Jokes aside, her uncensored nature has also led her to make some serious statements. Talking to *Elle* about the culture of Hollywood and its impossible standards, she said, "In Hollywood…I'm considered a fat actress."

Projecting a positive body image is something about which Jennifer is consistently mindful. "I'd rather look a little chubby on camera and look like a

actress on her natural, unmanipulated beauty—"I don't think that's Photoshop, that's you"—she cut him off at the knees, saying, "Of course it's Photoshop. People don't look like that!"

Jennifer's candor and humor have ingratiated her not only to fans, but to her co-stars and industry peers as well.

Jennifer reacts to an archery misfire during *The Hunger Games* press tour.

Jen visiting
Late Show
with David
Letterman in
2012.

person in real life than to look great on-screen and look like a scarecrow in real life," she told Canada's *Flare* magazine. "I like food…. I'm miserable when I'm dieting and I like the way I look. I'm really sick of all these actresses looking like birds."

While she's comfortable in her own skin, she admits that she's not as self-assured as some might think; she's got insecurities just like the rest of us. "That's just my voice, my very deep voice, which makes me sound confident," Lawrence joked to CNN.

Confidence or not, she doesn't seem to hold anything back—on any topic. She's even taken on *her own profession*. Talking to *Vanity Fair* in 2012, she said, "Not to sound rude, but [acting] is stupid. Everybody's like, 'How can you remain with a level head?' And I'm like, 'Why would I ever get cocky? I'm not saving anybody's life. There are doctors who save lives and firemen who run into

she said WHAT?!

"I love any TV that makes me feel better about myself."

Describing her love for trashy reality TV to Jay Leno

burning buildings. I'm making movies. It's stupid.'"

There's little doubt that the statement sent her publicists into a tizzy, but you have to admit, she *does* have a point. And even though our screen idols often seem larger than life, isn't it nice to see one come down to earth every once in a while?

Embarrassing Firsts

Meeting famous people can be, well, stressful. "Once I'm obsessed with somebody, I'm terrified of them instantly. I'm not scared of them, I'm scared of me and how I will react," Jennifer once told *Vanity Fair* magazine. Lest you think she's kidding, check out her embarrassing first encounters with these stars!

Daniel Radcliffe: Jennifer, like many of us, was a *Harry Potter* obsessive growing up. Not only had she read all the books (four times each!), but she'd even memorized several spells too. "I saw Daniel Radcliffe when I was doing *David Letterman* and I flipped out. I was *screaming*."

Embarrass-meter: 3 out of 4 grimaces

Meryl Streep: It's no secret Jennifer is an admirer of the veteran actress. She's often cited Streep as an artistic influence. So when Jennifer finally got up close and personal with one of her biggest idols, how'd it go? "Someone was introducing me to Bill Maher, and I saw Meryl Streep walk into the room, and I literally put my hand right in Bill Maher's face and said, 'Not now, Bill!' and I just stared at Meryl Streep."

Embarrass-meter: 2 out of 4 grimaces

Jack Nicholson: The actor ambushed her post-Oscar interview with ABC's George Stephanopoulos to praise her work in *Silver Linings Playbook*, giving his apologies for the interruption. "Yeah, you're being really rude," she said sarcastically. Jack, unfazed, went on to tell her that she reminded him of one of his old girlfriends. Not missing a beat, Jennifer cheekily replied, "Oh, really. Do I look like a *new* girlfriend?"

Embarrass-meter: 1 out of 4 grimaces

John Stamos: There's no arguing that Uncle Jesse was by far the dreamiest uncle on *Full House*. So meeting a childhood crush face-to-face, Jennifer was understandably...overwhelmed. "He was at a party, and I turned into a perverted guy. I was like following him into rooms and staring at his [backside].... He asked me if I was on mushrooms and I said, 'No, I'm dead sober. This is just *me*.'"

Embarrass-meter: 4 out of 4 grimaces

CHAPTER SIX

SILVER TURNS TO GOLD

Jennifer glows on Oscar night at the *Vanity Fair*–hosted after party.

It was an undertaking five years in the making. When the Weinstein Company optioned film rights to Matthew Quick's novel *The Silver Linings Playbook* in 2007, it originally intended for Sydney Pollack to direct and Anthony Minghella to produce the film. Pollack, unable to crack the script, then tapped controversial director David O. Russell to step in. A cavalcade of stars were attached, then unattached, to the film. But *Silver Linings Playbook* found a silver lining of its own in the 2013 awards season, when the movie sailed away with multiple honors, topped off with lead actress Jennifer Lawrence's win for Best Actress at the Academy Awards.

Jennifer was anything but a lock to play the part of Tiffany Maxwell. For one thing, the character was written to be much older than her. Scores of A-list actresses had been considered for the part—everyone from Rachel McAdams and Kirsten Dunst to Blake Lively and Rooney Mara. Anne Hathaway was even attached to the project for a time.

did you KNOW?

Silver Linings Playbook is the first movie since 1980's *Reds* to earn Oscar nominations in all four major acting categories. (Only Supporting Actress Maureen Stapleton took home a statuette, though Warren Beatty netted one for his direction.)

Perhaps even more impressive, *SLP* is the first movie in almost a decade to be recognized in all of the five major categories: Best Picture, Best Actor, Best Actress, Best Director, and Best Screenplay. (*Million Dollar Baby* was the last, winning Best Picture, Best Director for Clint Eastwood, and Best Actress for Hilary Swank.)

Jennifer had to lobby just to get an audition. Thankfully, Russell agreed to consider her—though the circumstances were less than ideal. The two linked up via Skype, the online video chat service, which would make the audition all the more impersonal. For their virtual meeting, Lawrence pulled out all the stops, decking herself out in an all-black wardrobe, her face slathered with goth makeup. She looked the part, at least. Reading lines across the Internet, Russell was blown away. After the audition, "it just seemed like there was no discussion to be had," the director told Deadline.com. "There was just something about her

that was…unparalleled. It was pretty remarkable, one of those 'stop the presses' kind of things."

But what about the fact that the 22-year-old would play a married-then-widowed woman? "We all wondered if she was too young, but she's someone who seems much wiser and older than she is. There's something you get from her eyes and her presence, that's remarkable and soulful," Russell told *USA Today*.

The story centers around two lost souls—Pat, a bipolar ex-teacher recently released from a mental institution, and Tiffany, a depressed

"**I think the essence of *Silver Linings* is heart. That's all the director cared about when we made the movie…. Because of that you have a movie that's filled with heartbreak and comedy, much like life.**"

—Bradley Cooper to *Entertainment Tonight*

Jennifer and Bradley Cooper in *Silver Linings Playbook.* Photo courtesy of AP Images

The legend and the newcomer: Robert De Niro and Jennifer stop for photographers at the 2013 Critics' Choice Movie Awards.

"When life reaches out to you, it's a sin not to reach back."

—Pat Sr. (Robert De Niro) in *Silver Linings Playbook*

and recently fired young widow—whose mutual vulnerabilities both repel and attract one another. The unconventional romance centers around a dance competition, a secret letter, and the delicate juju of the Philadelphia Eagles.

Delving into the complicated subject of mental illness was tricky territory for Russell, who also adapted the script. Russell, whose own son suffers from bipolar disorder, used his own family's struggles with the affliction to inform his script, calling it "deeply personal." Russell's close connection to the source material, and his dedication to portray bipolar disorder realistically and sensitively, was also what attracted Robert De Niro to the movie. The ultra-private De Niro told Katie Couric, "I don't like to get emotional, but I know exactly what [Russell] goes through," before breaking into tears.

The cast assembled, the key became developing the chemistry between the two romantic leads—Jennifer and co-star Bradley Cooper. They had never met but had quite the introduction: on the dance floor! "It's a great way to get to know a person. You're instantly sweating and learning something together," Lawrence said at the film's premiere. Jennifer credits the intensive dance rehearsals for establishing trust and an actors' shorthand between them. Whatever the reason, their characters' connection was palpable. "Bradley and I had really wonderful chemistry on screen. I think the key to...chemistry on screen is having no...chemistry off screen," Jennifer told the UK's *Sun*.

Jennifer goes dark as Tiffany in *Silver Linings Playbook.* *Photo courtesy of AP Images*

Jennifer admits that tackling the character of Tiffany was difficult. For starters, she had no one in her life to use as a reference point (her typical starting approach to a role). "I was very confused by her," Lawrence told the *Hollywood Reporter*. "She was just kind of this mysterious enigma to me because she didn't really fit any basic kind of character profile. Somebody who is very forceful and bullheaded is normally very insecure, but she isn't." Lawrence realized that Tiffany, at a base level, struggles because she accepts herself, but others don't. In Pat, she finally finds someone who is similarly misunderstood.

However much of a departure the character was from Lawrence's usual fare, she was still able to find some commonality with another iconic movie character. "It's funny. I never thought that Tiffany and Katniss have anything in common, other than they have to do what they have to do and really don't care what anybody thinks. However, the way they go about it is very different.

Personality TEST

Name: Tiffany Maxwell

Age: "Old enough to have a marriage and not wind up in a mental hospital."

Hometown: Philadelphia, PA

Nicknames: none that can be repeated here

Likes: the color black, people who are nonjudgmental

Dislikes: football—especially the Eagles

Hidden talent: I love to dance

How you get from here to there: jogging, usually

Philosophy: "There will always be a part of me that is dirty and sloppy, but I like that, just like all the other parts of myself."

Fun fact: I live in a garage—really!

by the NUMBERS $11,944

The amount raised at an auction for just five items from Jennifer's *Silver Linings Playbook* wardrobe. Not bad for a couple pieces of dancing clothes!

Katniss would rather not talk if she doesn't have to in every situation, and Tiffany has more words than there is time," Lawrence told Deadline.com.

Russell's script and direction, strong lead performances by Cooper and Lawrence, and brilliant supporting turns from De Niro, Jacki Weaver, and Chris Tucker, among others, proved to be the perfect combination. The film premiered at the Toronto International Film Festival and quickly snapped up the People's Choice Award for best picture. Critics were unabashed in their praise for the movie; theatergoers flocked to the film, making it one of 2012's sleeper successes.

The movie, though hard to pin down (is it a romantic comedy or a serious drama?) was a categorical triumph. Awards started coming in fast and furious. The film won best picture honors from scores of critics, including the American Film Institute, the Broadcast Film Association, Independent Spirit Awards, and the National Board of Review, among others. Jennifer picked up a number of awards along the way, too—winning big at the Golden Globes, Screen Actors Guild Awards, Independent Spirit Awards, and many more. Along the way, she never lost her trademark wit. (Joking at the Golden Globes, she thanked studio chief Harvey Weinstein "for killing whoever you had to kill to get me up here.")

On the biggest stage of them all, *Silver Linings Playbook* stormed the Oscars with eight nominations, third-most among all of the contenders. Among the film's nominations was a nod for its lead actress, considered the front-runner by Oscar oddsmakers.

By now, the play-by-play of Jennifer's charmed (and charming) Oscar night is well known. Tripping on her dress'

long train on the way to accept her award, Lawrence deftly deflected her embarrassment, saying, "You guys are just standing up because you feel bad that I fell...but thank you."

So the walk onstage might have been a cringe-worthy moment. Who cares? The silver lining—Oscar gold—was more than worth it.

Jennifer and Bradley became such good friends on *SLP* that they signed on to make not one but two new movies together.

CHAPTER SEVEN
GIRL ON FIRE

To have gone from her discovery on the streets of New York to Oscar's main stage in just a few short years is nothing short of remarkable. She's shown her range as an actress—she can do drama, comedy, action-adventure, and even horror (2012's *House at the End of the Street*) with equal aplomb—and she's demonstrated a veritable Midas touch when it comes to scripts, choosing one winner after the next. Jennifer, not her on-screen alter ego Katniss Everdeen, seems to be the *real* girl on fire.

With so much success in her already short career, it's a fair question to ask where she'll go from here. In the press room just moments after her triumphant Oscar win, one member of the press put it indelicately: "At 22 years old, you've got your first Oscar and you've already had two nominations. That's awfully young to have so much success so far…. You don't worry about peaking too soon?"

A question that could make other actresses weak in the knees, Jennifer brushed it off with a laugh: "Well, *now* I am!" But there was no time for worries with such a busy schedule. The day after the Academy Awards she was Katniss-brunette again, and headed back to Hawaii for *The Hunger Games: Catching Fire* reshoots. "I want to sit on my couch and drink and not change my pants for days at a time," she told E! on the Oscars red carpet. "Don't ask me about my schedule because I'm sinking into a bit of depression." Indeed, she has a full slate of projects coming up in the next year and shows no signs of taking a break from the madness.

"She spreads happiness wherever she is."

—Bradley Cooper to *USA Today* on his three-time co-star's charm

Jennifer gets spooked in *House at the End of the Street.*
Photo courtesy of AP Images

Chapter Seven Girl On Fire

In the midst of the wild success of *The Hunger Games* and *Silver Linings Playbook*, it's easy to forget that she's also headlined *another* huge action franchise: Marvel's *X-Men*. In 2014 she'll reprise her role as Raven (known better to comic book fans as Mystique) in *X-Men: Days of Future Past* alongside some undisputed heavyweights of the big screen. Indeed, the cast almost sounds like an awards-show roll call: Hugh Jackman, Ian McKellen, Michael Fassbender, Patrick Stewart, Peter Dinklage, James McAvoy, Ellen Page, and Halle Berry all star in the film, just to name a few. Fans of the first installment of director Bryan Singer's reboot, 2011's *X-Men: First Class*, should expect more thrills and spills, along with nuanced performances from the stars. Also, Jen's real-life BFF Zoe Kravitz and hotties Shawn Ashmore and Jen's ex-BF Nicholas Hoult reprise their *First Class* roles as mutant-students!

She's also set to reunite with her *Silver Linings* co-star Bradley Cooper in not one but *two* upcoming films. First up is *Serena*, a historical drama based on Ron Rash's novel of the same name. Set in Depression-era North Carolina, the story focuses on a timber baron (Cooper), his headstrong wife (Lawrence), and the greed, corruption, and secrets that tear them apart.

While the plot sounds like a bit of a departure from the lovefest that was *Silver Linings*, Cooper showed the love for Jennifer offscreen. Speaking to *Entertainment Tonight* about his co-star, he said, "I feel like I latched onto a secret before everybody knew about it. She's incredible…. I would do every movie with her."

And when David O. Russell came to each of them with his new project, the 1970s-set true-crime thriller *American Hustle*, they both said yes immediately, joining a cast rich with talent, from Christian Bale and Jeremy Renner to Louis C.K. and Amy Adams. Oh, and *SLP*'s Robert De Niro will join in on the fun too!

Director David O. Russell, Jennifer, and Bradley Cooper have joined forces again, for 2014's *American Hustle*.

"**My parents raised me to hold down a job. They instilled the work ethic in me. What this is, is a job, and that's what I'm doing, hopefully, my job. As far as jobs go, I'd say I was pretty lucky.**"

—Jennifer to *British Vogue* on how acting is work

Perhaps the most hotly anticipated project of all is the next installment of the *Hunger Games* movie franchise, *The Hunger Games: Catching Fire*. Picking up the story after Katniss and Peeta's dual win in the Hunger Games, the story will focus on the pair's victory tour and the brewing political rebellion. It also promises some juicier plot lines for rival love interest Gale.

While faithful readers of Collins' book know what to expect from the story, the latest trailers for the movie have hinted that there might be some unexpected elements too! Are we let in on President Snow and Plutarch Heavensbee's plot early on? Will the Quarter Quell play out like it does in the book? And what's with that K-I-S-S between Katniss and Gale? Fans will have to wait until November to find out.

Now an undisputed member of the exclusive Hollywood A-list, it seems she has the whole world in the palm of her hand and she can seemingly handpick any role she wants.

However, these days, she's tackling Hollywood's most difficult role: staying humble in the face of overwhelming fame and attention. "I don't ever walk

Jennifer shows off her new 'do at the GLAAD Media Awards in April 2013.

Hollywood Loves Jennifer!

Liam Hemsworth (*The Hunger Games*):
"She's one of the most energetic, fun-loving people I've ever met. Working with her on set is just easy.... She's amazing."

Julia Stiles (*Silver Linings Playbook*):
"I was so impressed with Jennifer Lawrence. She's really young, but she's so strong and formidable as an actress."

John Hawkes (*Winter's Bone*):
"[She's] a dedicated and interesting individual, and a talented actress and someone who is able to play some real heavy emotion, but the instant that they call 'Cut,' she can be back to her 18-year-old self. I thought she was a special human being, and, of course, she is. And I loved working with her."

Donald Sutherland (*The Hunger Games*):
"She's such a wonderful actress.... She should change her name to Jennifer Lawrence Olivier."

Josh Hutcherson (*The Hunger Games*):
"In a way I feel like I kind of am in love with Jennifer. She's such an amazing person, and she's obviously beautiful."

Woody Harrelson (*The Hunger Games*):
"She was raised well. Her folks are really cool. A lot of times people lose their heads when they get famous. It's because they're insecure. She's not insecure. You'd think arrogance comes from thinking too much of themselves, but it comes from thinking too little. She doesn't need to put on any airs. Her folks, her family, are all very important to her and she's always including them in her life. Her friends are really cool people. She's got her head screwed on pretty good."

Lenny Kravitz (*The Hunger Games*):
"I met Jennifer and, immediately, I fell in love with her. She's amazing, she's super funny at all times. She keeps you cracking up."

Bradley Cooper (*Silver Linings Playbook*):
"She doesn't seem like an actor. She's not narcissistic and it's not all about her. Even in the midst of promoting a movie, she's the same wherever she is, which is awesome. She makes you happy no matter what. She spreads happiness wherever she is. She's got her priorities. She gets it and knows what's important. You meet her parents and you know why right away. She keeps her family close to her."

The Girl on Fire stares down the competition.
Photo courtesy of AP Images

around feeling famous. I walk around feeling the exact same way I have walked around my entire life, but it's not until I talk to somebody and see in their eyes that I'm [perceived as] different. It makes me feel weird," she told *Marie Claire.*

She looks at Jodie Foster, her director in 2011's *The Beaver* as a role model in many ways, not least for her ability to remain totally unaffected by fame. "She's probably the most level-headed person I've ever met," Jennifer told *Interview* magazine. Observing the elder actress' qualities, Jennifer feels she has a blueprint: "I can do this and still be not just nice, but normal."

Jennifer was named one of *Time* magazine's 100 Most Influential People in the World in 2013—and was the magazine's cover subject, too. Foster authored Jennifer's profile, writing, "Sure, this girl can act. But man, this girl can also just be…. Jen's got it together." For an actress of Foster's caliber—and someone who's been in the business

this day in
HER-STORY
November 22, 2013

The Hunger Games: Catching Fire
premieres. Finally!

from an early age—to lavish such praise on Jennifer speaks volumes.

"I'm still in touch with reality and I see this business for what it is, which is a playground. I'm playing. I work at imagining things. None of this is real. None of this actually matters. I don't have a sense of superiority. I feel lucky but I don't feel special," Jennifer told *USA Today.* "The celebrity and fame thing and the acting part of it are two separate things. The celebrity part of it is so predictable. I'm not wowed by it," she continued. With an attitude like that, it seems certain that she'll make it in the business of Hollywood in the long term.

And what about aspirations beyond acting? She's acknowledged a desire to direct—someday. "I love acting, but I don't feel married to just being in front of the camera." Indeed, she's worked with some great female filmmakers already, including Foster and Debra Granik, who gave Jennifer her big break in *Winter's Bone*. "It has been inspiring for me to see really powerful, smart, strong women doing just as good of a job [as men]," she told *Interview*.

No matter what path Jennifer chooses, it seems success will surely follow. This girl's fire will be burning bright for years to come.

Looking ahead to the future, the outlook is bright.